HISTORY OF THE BODOS IN PHOTOGRAPHS

RITURAJ BASUMATARY

Contents

CHAPTER ONE

INTRODUCTION

The Bodos are one of the Indigenous People of North East India. They are the earliest settlers in North East India. The older generation of scholars used the term 'Bodo' to denote the earliest Indo- Mongoloid migrants to eastern India who subsequently spread over different regions of Bengal, Assam and Tripura.

Linguistically the Bodos include a large group of people who are the speakers of the Tibeto-Burman Speeches of the North and East Bengal, Assam and Burma. They are the Bodos or Boros of the Brahmaputra Valley, they are known as Meches in Lower Assam, West Bengal and Nepal and also known as Rabhas, Garos, Dimasas and Kacharis, Lalungs, Sonowals, Misings, Deuris, Chutias, Modahis, Ramcha, Thengal in Assam and Tipras in Tripura. Hence, Bodo is a general term, which is the generic name of the people, it means all the Tibeto-Burman (Bodo) speaking group of thc Sino Tibeto origin.

As per the classification given by Robert Snafer, in the Linguistic Survey of India describes the Boros or the Boro-Kacharis as a member of the Bodo (Boro) sub-section under the Assam Barma group of the Tibeto-Burman branch of the Sino-Tibeto-Chinese speech family.

The Bodo speaking areas of Assam at present are stretching from Dhubri in the West to Sodia in the East. In Tripura and Nagaland also a small number of the Boros or Boro-Kacharis are found to have been living. In Jalpaiguri and other adjacent districts of West Bengal, in Dimapur and adjacent areas of Nagaland, the Boros are known as Mech.

The Bodos, once were powerful and dominant race in the entire Northern and North Easter India are at present struggling for their barest existence. Racially, the Bodos, the earliest known ethnic group to inhabit to Assam (erstwhile Pragjyotishpur and Kamrupa) with their distinctive culture and linguistic traits belong to the Mongoloid stock of the Indo-Mongoloids or Indo-Tibetans.

CHAPTER TWO

RUINS OF KACHARI KINGDOM

CACHAR'S KHASPUR

The Kachari Ruins, Dimapur

Memories of Kachari kings--
Monolithic stone house at Maibang

CHAPTER THREE

KINGS, QUEENS AND HEROES OF KACHARI KINGDOM

Rulers

Dimapur

Virochana (835 – 885)
Vorahi (885 – 925)
Prasanto alias Prasadao (Chakradwaj alias Khamaoto) (925 – 1010)
Uditya (1010 – 1040)
Prabhakar (1040 – 1070)
Korpoordhwaj (1070 – 1100)
Giridhar (1100 – 1125)
Beeradhwaj (1125 – 1155)
Surajit (1155 – 1180)
Ohak (1180 – 1210)
Makardhwaj Narayan (Rana Pratap alias Raogena) (1210 – 1286)
Bhopal (1286 – 1316)
Purandar (1316 – 1336)
Bicharpatipha alias Prakash (1336 – 1386)
Vikramadityapha alias Vikaranto (1386 – 1411)
Mahamanipha alias Prabal (1411 – 1436)
Manipha (1436 – 1461)
Ladapha (1461 – 1486)
Khunkhora alias Khorapha (1486 – 1511)
Det tsang alias Dersongpha (1511 – 1536)

Maibang

Nirbhay Narayan (1540-c1550)
Durlabh Narayan or Harmesvar (c1550-1576)
Megha Narayana (1576–1583)
Satrrudaman (Pratap Narayan, Jasa Narayan) (1583–1613)
Nar Narayan (1613-)
Bhimdarpa Narayan (Bhimbal Konwar) (-1637)
Indraballabh Narayan (1637-)
Birdarpa Narayan (-1681)
Garurdhwaj Narayan
Makardhwaj
Udayaditya
Tamradhwaj Narayan (1699–1708)
Queen Chandraprabha

Suradarpa Narayan (-1730)
Dharmadhwaj Narayan (Harischandra Narayan)
Kirichandra Narayan (1735–1745)
Gopichandra Narayan (1745–1757)
Khaspur
Harischandra II (1757–1772)
Krishnachandra Narayan (1772–1813)
Gobindchandra Narayan (1813–1830 till of 14 August)
Tularam Hasnu (Till 1854 of 20 July)

JWHWLAO DAIMALU

THE KACHARI KING GOVINDA CHANDRA WITH HIS WIFE INDUPRABHA

SENGYAH TULARAM SENAPOTI
DATE OF BIRTH :11-03-1772
DATE OF DEATH : 12-10-1880

CHAPTER FOUR

BODO PEOPLE DURING BRITISH PERIOD

A PHOTO OF A BODO GIRL TAKEN DURING BRITISH ERA

A BODO GIRL WITH HER SIBLING

GROUP OF BODO MEN AND WOMEN DURING BRITISH PERIOD

BODO GIRLS PLAYING JEW'S HARP (GONGWNA/GOGONA)

CHAPTER FIVE

MUSICAL INSTRUMENTS OF THE BODOS

Various traditional musical Instruments of BODOS

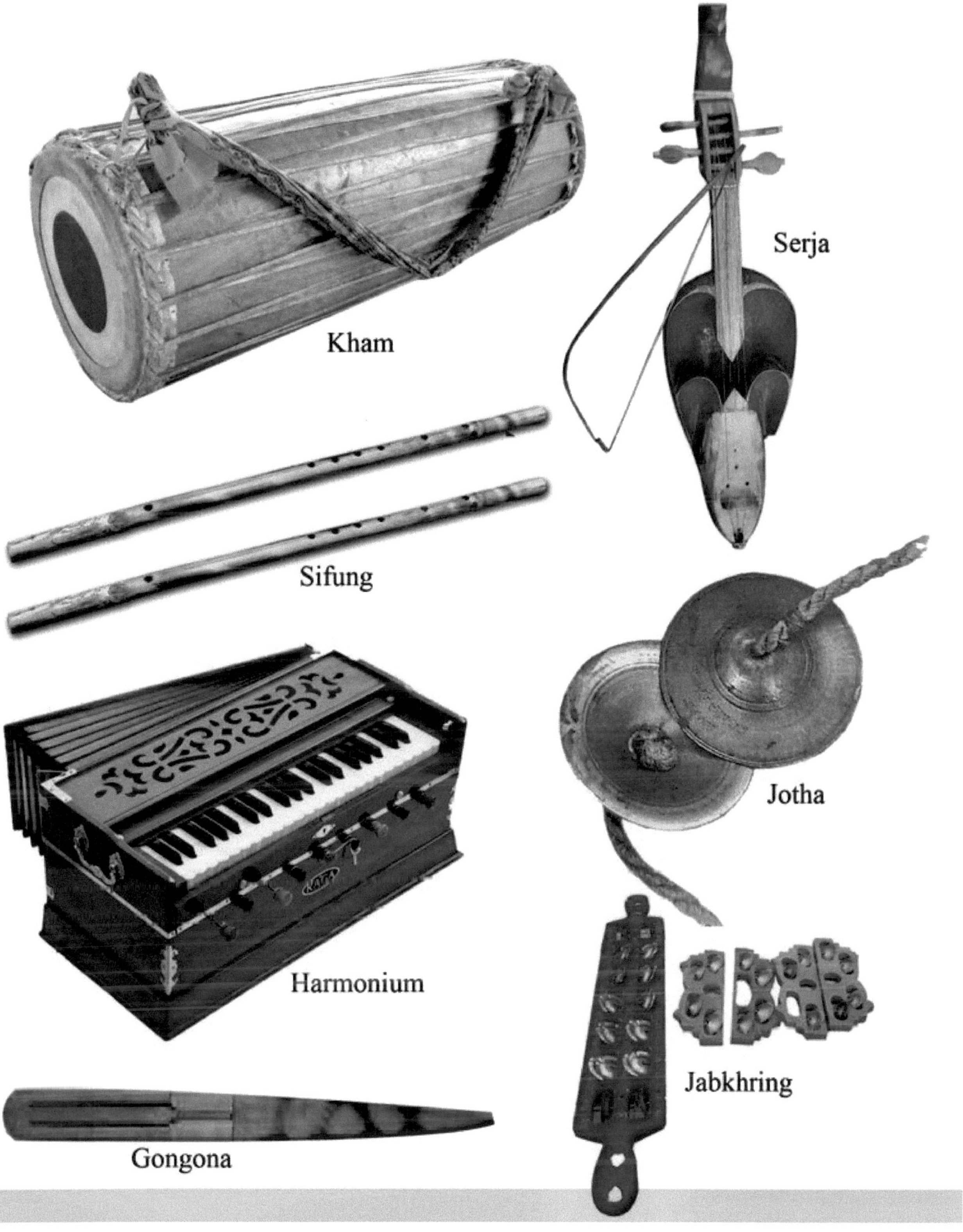

CHAPTER SIX

TRADITIONAL GAMES AND SPORTS OF THE BODOS

CLIMBING A BAMBOO PLANT

CLIMBING A BANANA PLANT

CHAPTER SEVEN

TRADITIONAL ART AND CRAFT OF THE BODOS

FISHING MATERIALS

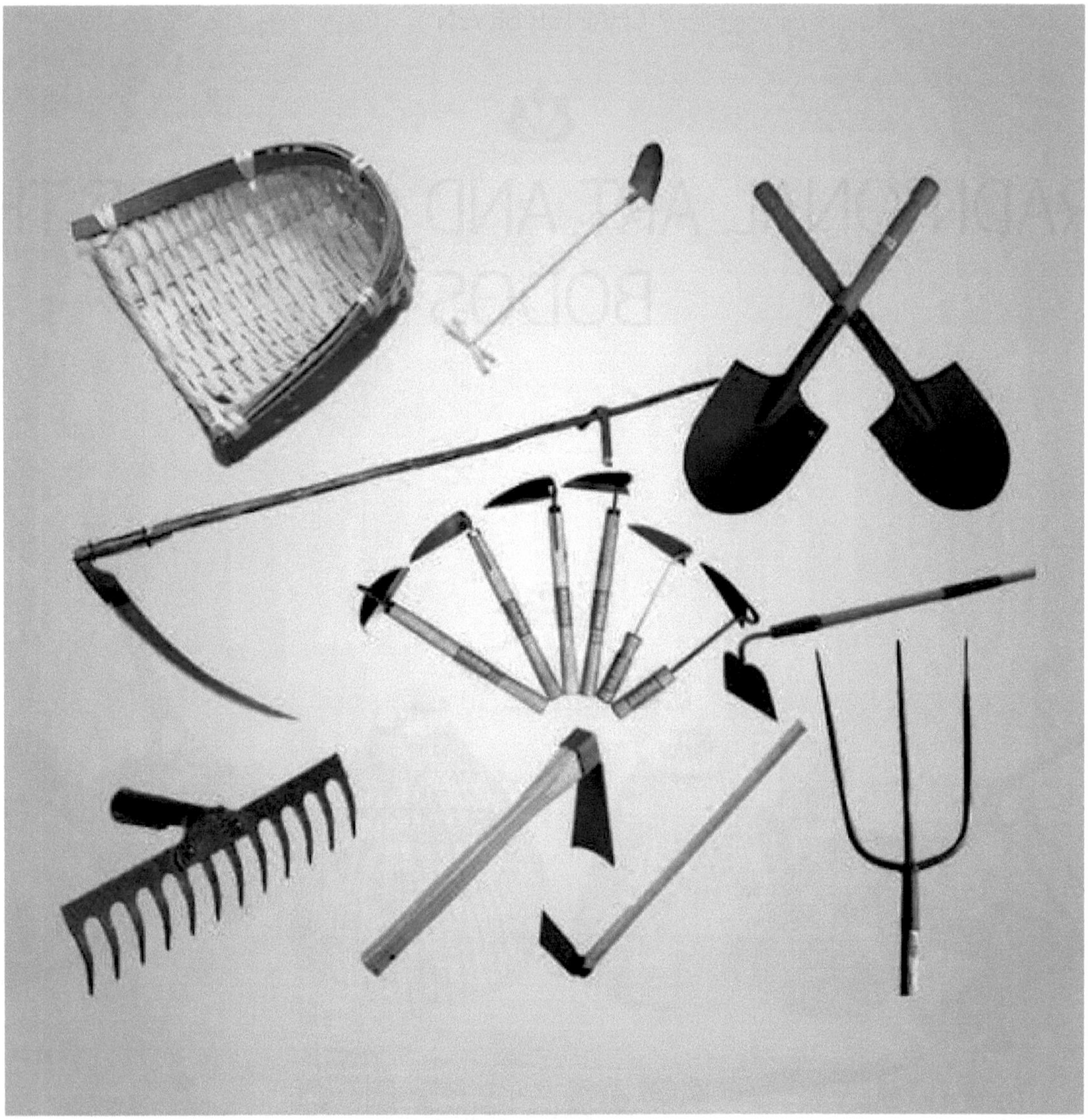

AGRICULTURAL TOOLS

CHAPTER EIGHT

TRADITIONAL BELIEF, FAIRS AND FESTIVAL OF THE BODOS

THE BATHOU ALTAR

BWISAGU FESTIVAL

BATHOU PUJA

CHAPTER NINE

TRADITIONAL DANCE OF THE BODOS

BAGURUMBA DANCE

DAHAL THUNGRI SIBNAI DANCE

BARDWI SIKLA DANCE

CHAPTER TEN

SCENE OF THE BODO VILLAGES

CHAPTER ELEVEN

SOCIAL REFORMER AND FREEDOM FIGHTERS FROM BODO COMMUNITY

Left to right(Standing) : Baburam Brahma, Karendra Narayan Mandal(Brahma).
Left to right(Sitting) : Jadav Chandra Khakhlari, Subedar Belbungram Kachari, Mohd. Giasuddin Ahmed(Advocate)
Sitting on the ground : Gurudev Kalicharan Brahma

Group photograph taken after meeting the Simon Commission at Shillong on January 4, 1929

Satish Chandra Basumatary (16 November 1901 – 16 November 1974) was an Indian Bodo poet, dramatist, Social worker and the second president of Bodo Sahitya Sabha. He is a pioneer people of Bibar era, the age of renaissance of Bodo literature. He is credited with helping established Bodo Brahma Dharma. He was also the editor of first Bodo magazine Bibar in 1924. He was honoured Mengnw Rwngwi Jwhwlao title after his death.

Rupnath Brahma (1902-1968) was a Bodo poet, politician and religious scholar. He was born on 15 June 1902 at Owabari village of Kokrajhar district. He was the son of Dhajendra Brahma and Khwdwmsri Brahma. He breathed his last on 23 January 1968. He is credited with helping establish Brahma Dharma. His poems were mostly mystic in character. He was also first minister from the Bodos. The Inter-State Bus Terminal of Guwahati is named after him to commemorate him as Rupnath Brahma Inter-State Bus Terminal.

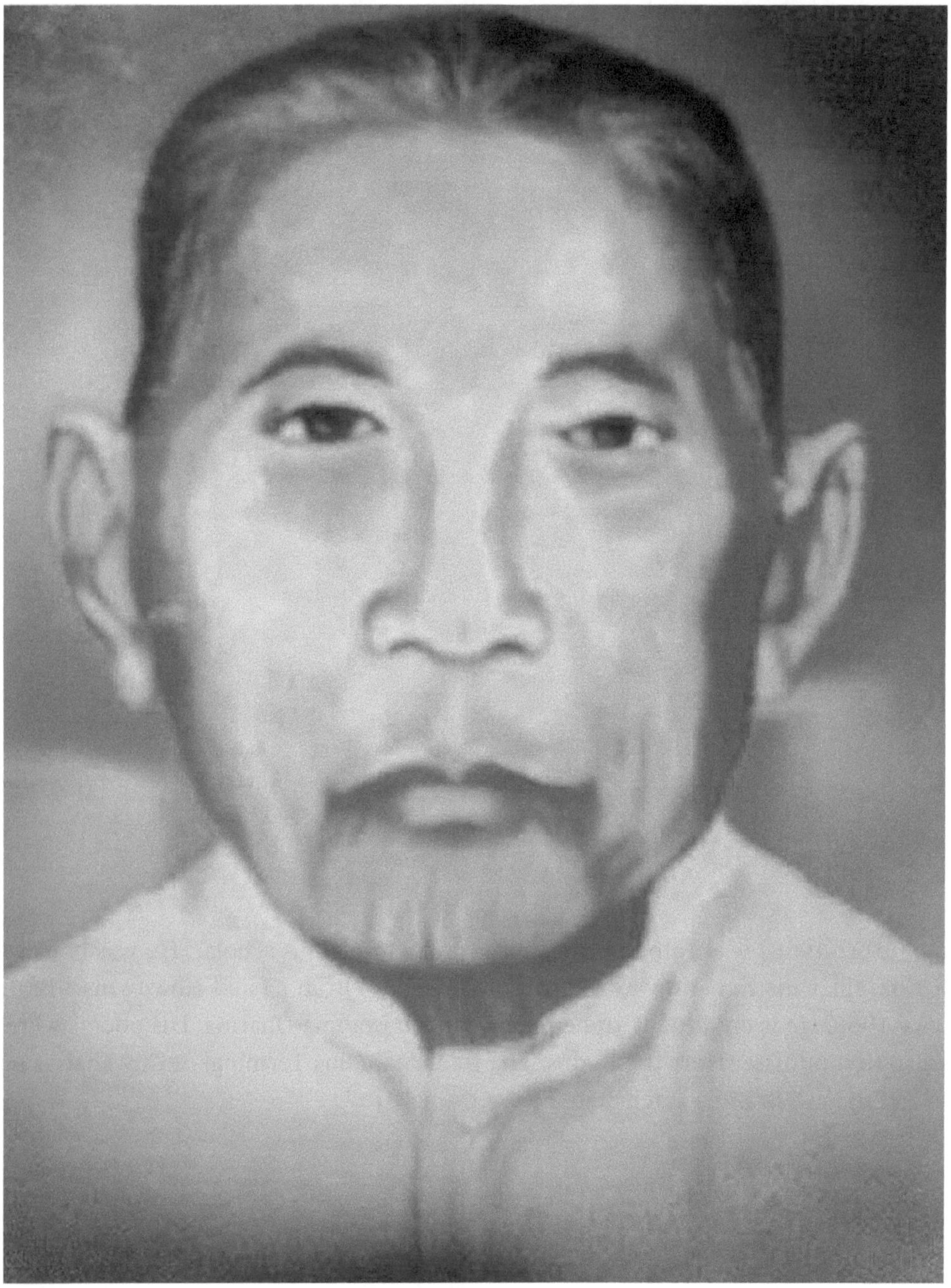

Madaram Brahma was an Indian poet and dramatist, who wrote in the Bodo language, a Sino-Tibetan language spoken by the Bodo people. Born in a Bodo family in 1903 at Kokrajhar in Dundhunikhata (present day Dhubri District) of the Northeast Indian state of Assam, he passed the matriculation from the local Government High School in Dhubri. His career started as a teacher and by 1932, he became the Headmaster of the Harisingha High School, Darang. In 1945 he joined the local administration, eventually becoming the first person of Bodo ethnicity to become a Block Development Officer.

Jogendra Kumar Basumatary (19 May 1920- 28 March 2010) was an Indian writer and social worker from Bodo community. He was elected as a president of Bodo Sahitya Sabha held in 1983. He received the first U.N. Brahma Soldier Humanity Award in 2004.

He was born on 19 May 1920 at Gosaigaon village under Manikpur circle, in Goalpara district (present Kokrajhar) of Assam. He was the son of Arindra Basumatary and Gilashri Basumatary. He breathed his last on 28 March 2010.

Jogendra Kumar Basumatary was not only a writer and social worker but also a freedom fighter. Police arrested him twice for participating in the freedom struggle. During Quit India movement, he was arrested and jailed for 6 moths at Guwahati jail.

After independence, he was honoured with Tamrapatra by the Central Goverment and granted him pension in 1973. The Assam Goverment honoured him in 1993. The State Goverment also gave him literary pension for his valuable contribution to the Bodo literature. The Upendranath Brahma Trust (UNBT) also honoured him with its first UN Brahma Soldier of Humanity Award for his immense contribution in all fields during 2004.

CHAPTER TWELVE

PLAINS TRIBAL COUNCIL OF ASSAM (PTCA) AND DEMAND FOR UDAYACHAL

CHAPTER THIRTEEN

ROMAN SCRIPT MOVEMENT

The Roman script movement, which was launched by the Bodo Sahitya Sabha in 1974, involved the whole Bodo community all over the state of Assam followed by massive police operations in all the Bodo-dominated areas, resulting in untold miseries of the people.

Martyrs List

Amla Ram Boro	:	Barpeta Road
Siba Ram Boro	:	Barpeta Road
Haitha Ram Basumatary	:	Phakhriguri (Kokrajhar)
Bistu Ram Basumatary	:	Halowadal (Kokrajhar)
Dina Nath Boro	:	Bijini
Kanteswar Goyary	:	Bijini
Malsingh Goyary	:	Bijini
Budhbar Boro	:	Bijini
Kanchai Boro	:	Bijini
Pani Ram Daimary	:	Ruwta (Darrang)
Sambar Mushahary	:	Udalguri
Anjeush Raglary	:	Udalguri
Nidhi Ram Basumatary	:	Ramphalbil (Kokrajhar)
Narayan Narzary	:	Ramphalbil (Kokrajhar)
Ajendra Basumatary	:	Ramphalbil (Kokrajhar)
Narayan Basumatary	:	Kokrajhar

MARTYRS OF ROMAN SCRIPT MOVEMENT

CHAPTER FOURTEEN

FIRST WAVE OF BODOLAND MOVEMENT

BODOFA UPENDRA NATH BRAHMA

FLAG AND SYMBOL OF ALL BODO STUDENTS UNION

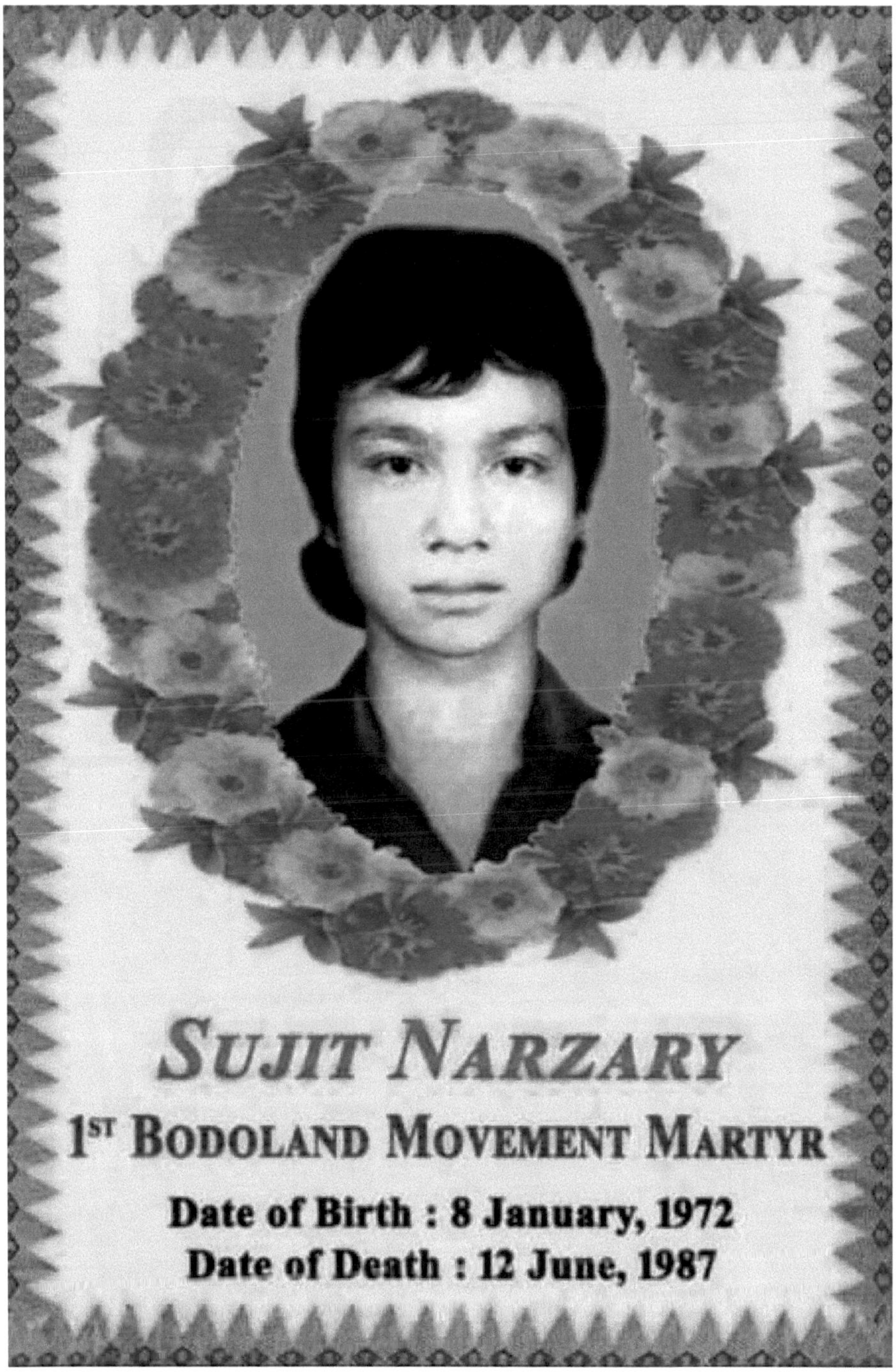
SUJIT NARZARY
1ST BODOLAND MOVEMENT MARTYR
Date of Birth : 8 January, 1972
Date of Death : 12 June, 1987

BAC ACCORD 1993

CHAPTER FIFTEEN

SECOND WAVE OF BODOLAND MOVEMENT

Bodo Liberation Tigers Force

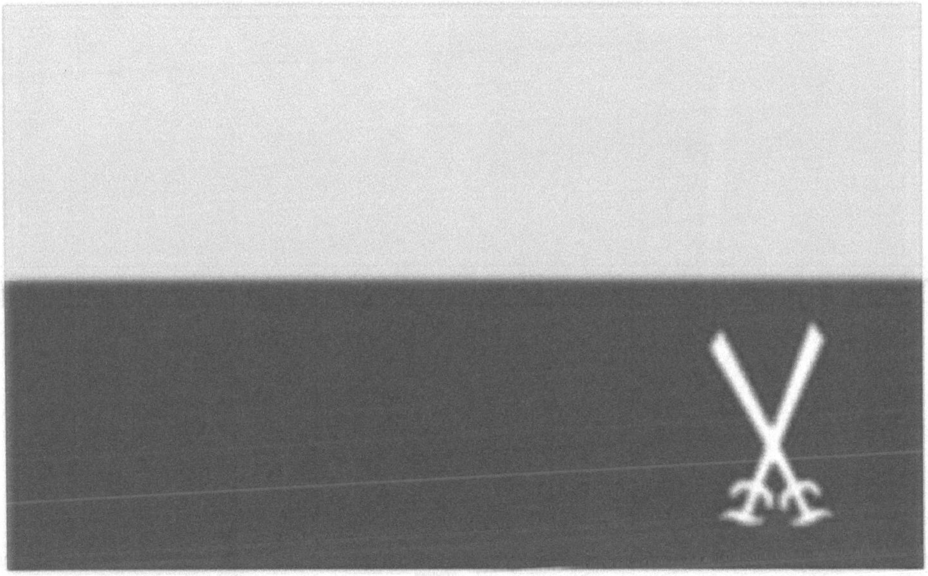

Flag of the Bodo Liberation Tigers Force

BTC ACCORD 2003

CHAPTER SIXTEEN

THIRD WAVE OF BODOLAND MOVEMENT

National Democratic Front of Boroland

National flag of Boroland used by NDFB

SYMBOL OF NDFB

BTR ACCORD 2020

CHAPTER SEVENTEEN

FOURTH WAVE OF BODOLAND MOVEMENT

CHAPTER EIGHTEEN

CONCLUSION

History says, the Bodos are the aboriginals of Assam. They once ruled Assam till around 1854 A.D. They belong to the Indo-Mongoloid stock and their language is derived from the Assam Burmese branch of Tibeto Burman sub-family.

Printed by Libri Plureos GmbH in Hamburg,
Germany

9 798888 335987